Turner

Vasile   Nicolescu

ABBEY LIBRARY
LONDON

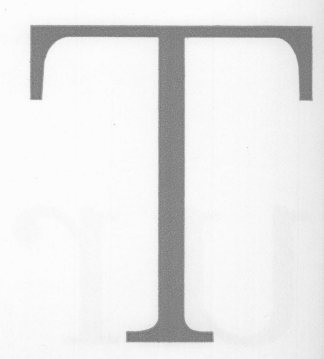

urner

Translated from Romanian as published by
MERIDIANE PUBLISHING HOUSE
Bucharest, 1976
under the original title of
TURNER

Translated into English by
DAN DUŢESCU

I'm tied to the high mast like Ulysses.
Tritons and dolphins rend me one by one.
And yet my eyes can see beyond all dreams
the light alighting from an unseen sun.

I'm pierced through by the shot of pelting snow;
dead seagulls come to crash against my breast.
As my sad eyes balance the high noon, lo,
I'm like a shaft of ice, a crimson mast.

The sun's grit burns and kindles up my face.
A torch I am within a vault of clouds.
The play of lightning, fearfully ablaze,
changes my sea to burning pyres of hues.

A cloud I am, gold ashes in the blast,
a living water-lily, eye agleam.
Chimeric suns are gathered in my sight,
the heavy light that lies beyond all dreams.

VASILE NICOLESCU
Translated by DAN DUȚESCU

A PRELUDE TO TURNER

I. THE MYTH OF COLOUR

There is a restrained exasperation of colour in Turner, a subdued frenzy, amplified down to the depths, irreducibly dramatic from its very beginnings. Unlike his great forerunner and "rival", never absent from his thoughts, the classic Claude Lorrain, in whose paintings things are both haloed and petrified by the sun, unlike his persistent yet quiet bias for the mythologically solar fairyland, with a-temporal geological constructions, Turner is a burning visionary, a prodigiously great poet of colour for his time. His early partiality for giant forms, for super-dimensions, should not be suspected of artificiality or mimetism — as one of his fastidious commentators, Kenneth Clark, tries to insinuate. With Turner everything is an occasion for inner confrontation, a confrontation at a very high level and sublimely pretentious. The Lorrainian motifs of his beginnings will pursue him, not without profit, to the end of his life, despite all the metamorphoses that his art will undergo, despite the variety of themes and techniques in his painting. Is not this impression fully illustrated by The Visit to the Tomb, a picture of mythological inspiration representing Dido making her way to Sychaeus' sepulchre, a work completed in 1850, that is, a year before his death? Above all, however, the artist is a sensitive master of colour, an alchemist of its virtues, fully aware of his own visionary possibilities, of his capacity to express and incorporate in colour the drama of the real. The obsession of yellow, for example, the iridescent gold of his palette speak rather of the artist's transfigurative vision, his power, characteritic of his temperament, to grasp, introvertly, the inner spasm of nature, its painful commotions, the secret agony and epic of matter in its ceaseless motion. The gold that creeps into his paintings, drawings and watercolours, from the most imperceptible iridescence to violent hues, is rather a symbolic colour, a colour of subtle convergences, of sublime mysterious consumptions, dramatically existential. Keenly perceptive like later on Cézanne before nature, Turner is no less pervaded by dream vision representations like Coleridge, is possessed in no lesser degree by the sense of levitation, by the aerial élan peculiar to the visionary Shelley, is not devoid of a certain Titanism characteristic of Romanticism. Restless and alive, Turner's landscape work covers with its substance all such areas of dream. A grave, symphonic theme with variations his creation seems to be, in which colours become eddies of sounds, cries of terror before the unfettered elements, in which the blinding snowstorms and the nocturnal fireworks clearly express Nature's great convultions, indomitable and cruel, threatening the feeble, frail human being. Turner's Prometheanism — an expression of the same romantic fire — is there in all the dramatism, sometimes paroxysmal, of his seascapes with shipwrecks, cyclones and snowstorms. In them the human being, even when overcome by despair — as in the famous Shipwreck exhibited in 1805 — or when it assumes tragic dimensions — as in The Slave Ship — vibrate with tension and anxiety.

Sensitive to the lesson learned from his studio companion, Girtin, receptive to the techniques used by the creators of the "classical sublime", Cozens and William, overwhelmed by the colouristic craftsmanship of a Lorrain or a Poussin, passing through his own filters the experience of the great and "lesser" Dutch artists as well as, later on, the vigorously didactic experience of a Canaletto or a Guardi, reproducing from memory drawings and watercolours of abbeys and castles, travelling through England, wandering along shores and across seas, living like an "écorché vif" through the experience of tempest, chasm, and impending death, climbing the giddy heights of the Alps and brightened up by the candid, unreal sun of Spoleto or the Venetian lagoon, Turner develops an extraordinary sense of nature. Ruskin, M. Brion reminds us, said that Turner treated the rocks "with the same simplicity of light and shade as a great portrait painter would treat the human face" or that "in front of his drawings a geologist might give a lecture on the theory of erosion". The French aesthetician drew the conclusion that the artist "had acquired the knowledge of nature empirically, instinctively, by divining the formation of rocks when he was drawing them, by sensing the mysterious drama of our planet, of the convultions of its

Alps, of their rise and fall. The sketches made at Mer de Glace, Chamonix, are of an impressive, tragic vivacity". Paradoxically, as his knowledge grew more exact, more scientific, more objective, his visions became more impetuous and free, more subjective and pure. So much the more extraordinary was his sense of colour, a sense which he cultivated with heroic tenacity. To penetrate the mystery of colour was for him to find a vehicle, necessary to his temperament, an adequate language for expressing the latent volcanism, the organic Romanticism, the unsuspected depths of his spirit. Colour is a reality and a myth, an absorbing force, inwardly centrifugal, the purest revealer of his own essence, of his interiority. The deeper the artist plunges into the mystery of colour, the higher his visionary state. Turner did not make hundreds of studies of clouds like John Constable, his contemporary (the first British landscape painter to be acknowledged in Paris) in order to discern in their interplay the inconstancy, transitoriness and fugacity, the gliding and fluidity of matter. In spite of that, I do not know of more evanescent, purer clouds, more eloquently Impressionistic, hovering just above an ocean of dew than the clouds in his watercolours at the British Museum *or at the* Municipal Museum *and* Art Gallery *of* Birmingham. *And never before have I contemplated clouds like those in* Snowstorm: Hannibal and his Army Crossing the Alps *or in his well-known* Snowstorm at Sea *of 1842, eddying clouds, apocalyptically coloured, clouds of the primordial chaos, charged with tragic, impassioned, devastating electricity. The clouds seem to have the density of metal fluids, whizzing clouds, visiting our planet for the first time.*

Turner's predilection for yellow *(a predilection which some of his contemporaries censured harshly) seems to be associated, as in the case of Van Gogh, with a certain type of tragic vision. 'How beautiful yellow is!' had once exclaimed the artist who had painted the flamboyant suns and cypresses of Arles; 'but how tragic these suns engendering vertigos, engendering questions without answers!' Indeed, how beautiful, how sublime is Turner's yellow, that yellow infused into the waterspouts, the sunset clouds, the gap between Alpine rocks, the morning clouds wrapping the sea in which monsters are teeming. That yellow seems however to lie concentrated at the root of things, to look towards us past the elements with the strange force of a half extinguished sun and to irradiate a tragic, puzzling, esoteric light. While Lorrain's yellow has the softness of velvet and covers with a golden varnish columns, trees, sunsets, figures emerging from legends, imparting to them an ecstatic appearance, it acquires with Turner the value of a fundamental colour, a coagulant of both atmosphere and significance. A demiurge of the landscape, Turner puts this colour into the pores of stones, into the space between archways, into the pulp of trees and into people's clothes, into the rustling foliages and into the heart of the flames, into the rocks of the cliffs and into the haze of the rising sun. Sulphur yellow, citron yellow, yellow with an orange mute, mat yellow or bright, transparent or with the most unexpected gradations of colour, it often has a counterpoint significance: the blind sun in* Hannibal and his Army Crossing the Alps *. . . is more of a luminary for calvary; the sun in* Staffa: Fingal's Cave *emblematically placed on the sea's dark horizon enhances the atmosphere of latent anxiety, visited by chimeras, of the legendary Ossianic shore; the blood-red streamers in* The Burning of the Houses of Lords and Commons *float over surges of yellow clouds (a thing visible particularly in the watercolour made a year before in preparation for this canvas); the light in the celebrated* Interior at Petworth *except that in the centre, more spectral and of a strangely opalescent shade, is of a steamy, vegetal yellow, outlining a world ravaged by apparitions; the light witnessing* The Parting of Hero and Leander *only enhances even more the characters' feeling of solitude and gloomy premonition of death. It is the feeling that hovers over* The Shipwreck *as well: inclined masts, a paroxysmal suggestion of destruction and disaster, the superhuman attempt by the oarsmen in the two boats to come near the shipwreck in their boat, everything is caught in a merciless yellow spotlight, like a supreme seal of the frozen pallor that is to come. Rejecting sentimentalism and effusions apt to wilt under various academizing canons, he pushed, with exemplary boldness, the language of painting almost one century forward. Yellow is over the greatest part of his work a starting point colour and a corollary colour. Yellow lights up obsessively the human being's core. It is a colour of confession, a verb-colour, born as if to illustrate the hallucinations in Aloysius Bertrand's* Gaspard de la nuit *or Lautréamont's "the Ocean's apostrophes" in* Maldoror's Chants. *All this range of impressions made by Turner's yellow strikes most of the examiners of his paintings, giving the feeling of a diffuse theory, subtly insinuated, yet the more soul-stirring. Thus Mayoux, the author of an accurate* Introduction to English Painting, *stops for a while in front of the fantastic canvas* Sunrise with a Sea-Monster *and, without doing too much psychoanalysis (like Jack Lindsay, an important biographer of Turner) states, " . . . we then have* Sunrise with a Sea-Monster *in which, at last, the confession of the obsession must somehow appear. The monster is a Leviathan in the image* of a deep-sea fish, with two enormous eyes against the sulphur-yellow of the sunrise." It is also the impression it made on us in one of the rooms of the museum on the bank of the Thames. The canvas, seen from a distance, is a symphony in yellow, apparently restful or calm, but contemplated from a normal distance the marine "nightmare" appears terrifying, obsessive. The yellow becomes the expression of primordial chaos, a symbol of genesis also, perhaps, because of the film of sulphur vapours, of the imperceptible "tourbillon" motion of the light. The feeling is one of dream-like, hallucinatory sea captivity. A "cinerama" in oil? You are a prey to an incredible sensation. You find it difficult to rouse yourself from the reverie, you walk away with your head turned towards the picture and you feel like brushing away the vapours off your eyes and off your clothes.

Naturally, in his vast work Turner did not reject the fairy-tale atmosphere or the light tones in which the range of yellow acquires yet other values, other distributions and aesthetic implications. As is the case with his rich series of watercolours where he acted like a true magician and in which the virtuoso, vying with the poet, has left an inestimable legacy of brief, feverish notations, spontaneous representations corresponding to the most varied states of mind. It is not our intention to exhaust analytically the infinite scope of aesthetic meaning of his yellow and much less his chromatic range in general by a unilateral and inevitably simplifying reduction to one element alone. We have dwelt however at some length on it because, after direct research into his work, it has imposed itself upon us as having a more profound categoric value which can reveal a structure, an evolution. The artist himself granted it special attention. Witness to this are some of his "diagrams" of colour also exhibited at The Tate Gallery and, in the field of theory, his annotations to Goethe's treatise The Science of Colour in which the artist did not conceal his gratification at discovering that he saw eye to eye with the poet of Weimar in this respect.

II. THE DRAMATURGY OF LIGHT

Turner is one of the few colourists, if not the only one, who had the straightforward ambition to recompose on canvas the illusion and miracle of the aurora borealis, to suggest to us, by a simple and delicate spreading of colour, its magnificent irreality, its purifying presentiment. A dramaturge of light, the artist felt intensely the need to and the hope of unfettering it. By overturning the real into the depths of dreaming, he raised in fact dreaming to the heights of the real. By decanting fleeting impressions, subliming sensations, superimposing the colours with a technique which has remained unknown to this day, operating with that visionary impression, as was said, characteristic of his art, Turner subordinated his sensibility to that painful urge to snatch the light from colour, to give it the vivacity, the freshness, the relief and the power of expression of truth itself. Achieving huge panels in which colourful landscape, drawing-landscape or imaginary landscape co-exist, with a thrilling inner freedom of the mythological or historical types (unaffected by the charge of conventionalism attributed a priori to this genre by Baudelaire in the pages devoted to the Salon of 1846), the artist was permanently concerned with the mystery of colour. The dramatism of his visions was always organically in tune with the dramatism of these pursuits. Turner never started from ready-made solutions, conveniently utilizable and when after 1830 he was turning more and more obviously towards the abstracting of colours, his move was a conclusion and a beginning, an ascending continuation, raising his art and modern art in general to a superior level. Much has been said and yet too little about the contribution of his art to the development of Impressionism. The English critics, with the exception of the great Ruskin, defined their attitudes late enough. French criticism, partisan and conservative, sooner accepted Constable as an innovator. Only the artists themselves, brilliant representatives of Impressionism, Renoir, Pissarro, Sisley, Monet and others, in the well-known letter sent to Coutts Lindsay, after pointing out that their aim was " to interpret shape in motion as well as the fleeting phenomena of light ", felt it necessary to confess simply "that they cannot forget that they were preceded, in this respect, by a great master of the English school, the illustrious Turner". Moreover, some time later, the Neo-Impressionist Paul Signac considered Turner close even to the severe technique of the diffusion of colour, of its elaborate stippling cultivated by the Pointillists. (As a matter of fact the English word "stippling" means nothing else but "Pointillism"). The supreme argument regarding the striking novelty and modernity of Turner's painting is offered to the same Paul Signac by the book of the American O. N. Rood "A Scientific Theory of Colour", in which the English artist appears as an extraordinary master of the gradation of colour technique.

This inclination for analysis, this voluptuousness of an alchemist of colour are connected in Turner with the quality of his talent, his temperament and his personality. His impulse comes strictly from within, it is not one of accomodation, not an impersonal welcome to a fashion. The fact is demonstrated by most of his sketches which have been preserved in an impressive number (19,000 drawings and sketches) in the section of prints of the British Museum. *Pursuing the effects of shadow and light even in the diagrams dedicated to perspective (of which we observe the drawing of a "Doric frieze" and the watercolour representing "two glass balls partly filled with water"), Turner is an artist who studies thoroughly in permanent connection the most diverse techniques of proportion, contrast, rhythm, "éclairage" and gradation of colour. Associated with a frantic participation, with a deep awareness of reality, they give wings to his boundless imagination. He does not transfigure the ephemeral sensation but fathoms and fixes in a deeply personal interpretation an essential quality which belongs to the eternal quality of things.*

Nor does he, in watercolours, allow himself an easy-going attitude of mere spontaneity, at least such as was imposed by tradition. In this respect, too, he is an innovator, a revolutionary, who discontinues the technique of strictly and obligatorily applying the drawing in pencil before the watercolour proper. The watercolours made after his first journey to Italy (1819), as for example Venice, looking East from the Giudecca at Sunrise, *then his matchless* Buildings by a Lake *(1840—1845) are performed with extremely delicate washes of pure, transparent colour, to which the "strokes", also white, of the brush-stem or the finger nail are associated in order to enhance the play of water reflexions. In the watercolours* Boats at Sea, *perhaps the most modern in our opinion, one is struck by the simplicity of the motif: two delicately vertical spots emerging from the centre of the median horizontal line of the picture — two mere strokes of black and vermilion covering symmetrically the horizon and the sea — achieve the whole translucent unity of the lanscape, its dream-like depth.*

The same transfigurative power irradiates simultaneously in the other section of his work, his oil-paintings. Most relevant from the same point of view is the analysis made by Signac of the last variant, the 1835 one, of Norham Castle: Sunrise, *with reference to the earlier picture dated 1815. To the descriptive character, the redundancy of colour, the intricacy of detail in the first form is now opposed, with absolute superiority, a pictorial subtlety, soul-stirring in its suggestiveness: " . . . a large spot of yellow in the middle of a sky, blending into the lilac hue of the two sides in a perfect gradation of colour. In the middle, an indefinite spot of blue: the castle and its reflexion without any architectural details. On the left, a smear of purple trickles into the orange where no object is clear, only some darker violet suggesting a roof. On the right, a gradation of colour in two shades, one yellow, one violaceous. In the middle of the water, reflecting the sky, a red spot . . .".*

All his life Turner ascended a prodigious spiral whose top step was the yellow colour; he had then the awesome sensation of touching, of feeling the cosmic white, a pure synthesis of all colours, the ultimate truth, light. And the drama of its unfettering takes possession of him, especially, in the last few years of his life, with increasing passion.

His tragic vision puts ever more frequently its seal on many of his late canvases and watercolours: Light and Colour *(1840),* The Angel standing in the Sun, Undine giving the ring to Masaniello *(1846) or even* Skeleton falling off a Horse *(1830), in which the colours gravitate towards a swirling luminescent nucleus, a chasm of light tending to absorb the whole being into an open space, all of it giving a dizzying sensation. By handling these seemingly abstract hues, by absorbing and dissolving ever more the contour in order to communicate more, by liberating light, the artist liberates himself, in a secret, composed, discreet apotheosis. The wing of darkness touches him, hesitatingly too, on a December morning: Turner dies while watching the sun.*

ANTHOLOGY OF TEXTS

...but we have not yet learned to look back again at this magnificent giant of English painting — a lonely giant, perhaps, with no great following, but none the less perhaps the greatest we have.

HERBERT READ

He first perfected himself in the typically English art of watercolour, and he became the greatest master the world has ever known of this particular *genre*.

HERBERT READ

But in fact two artists of genius, one at the beginning, and one at the end of the century, show that the landscape of fantasy was still a valid and potent means of expression. They are Turner and Van Gogh. Both are fundamentally northern artists — painters of midnight sun and the aurora borealis. Yet both are inspired by the landscape of Mediterranean countries, because only in these could they find that delirium of light which was the release of their emotions.

KENNETH CLARK

The landscape assumes all the aspiration of the heart; it is the boundless field of poetic freedom; and, a priviledged crossroads of moods, it even ceases to be a type in order to become the sole necessity of a generation for which romanticism is neither a fashion nor an aesthetics but a gush from the depths of one's being, a constant exaltation of life and of the eye!

HENRI LEMAÎTRE

Turner is an exception to all rules, and can be judged by no standard of art. In a wildly magnificent enthusiasm, he rushes through the ethereal dominions of the world of his own mind — a place inhabited by the *spirits of things;* he has filled his mind with materials drawn from the close study of nature (no artist has studied nature more intently) — and then changes and combines, giving effects without absolute causes, or, to speak more accurately, seizing the soul and essence of beauty, without regarding the means by which it was effected.

JOHN RUSKIN

Having succeeded in rising above the emotional and contemplative origin of his art in order to conceive painting as a search for what is intimate, profoundly real and dispassionate in nature, Turner can be considered the first truly modern painter of Europe.

GIUSEPPE GATT

Everything is mystery and mirage in the life as well as in the work of this painter. His art is the meeting point of a discipline still feeding on classicism and of that disposition of the English temperament which is expressed in a propensity towards dreaming, even towards phantasmagoria and whose concrete result is the outward projection, with an indiscribable power of achievement, of the inner world. With a perseverance which is almost a monomania, Turner turns out image after image, crystalized not round the elements of the visible world, but wrought by his imagination.

G. OPRESCU

...a visionary... he launched himself into a series of astounding anticipations of later conquests. With an extremely varied palette and a brush disregarding the

Study

restrictive notions of form or contour, he painted pictures bathed in a dazzling brightness similar to iridescent mirages.

RENÉ HUYGHE

(Turner, ed.) who would be the Lord of all.

CONSTABLE

The light pervading his paintings is not a calm light, but one in motion, with explosions, with all kinds of quaint glitterings. He first adopted a gloomier range of colour which little by little he clarified, volatilized, dissolved and which towards the end of his life he presented like matter in fusion.

G. OPRESCU

In terms borrowed from another visionary artist, Victor Hugo, one has often spoken of "the mouth of shade" and "the gulf of shade". Here however *(Interior of Petworth,* ed.) is "the mouth of light", "the gulf of light".

J. J. MAYOUX

Transforming his vision, giving it a more and more unreal background, he comes towards the end of his life to paint nothing else but the light in a sort of continual and varied apotheosis.

G. OPRESCU

He expresses the cosmic drama by means of the magic of light.

JEAN LEYMARIE

Everything that is material or suggesting matter has evaporated; all we have before us are phantoms of light, which no longer correspond in any way with realities, seen through an iridescent haze. Here and there a livelier note, a boat, a fragment of architecture, volume and colour a little more persistent; the rest of the picture being rendered in the form of evanescent vapours.

G. OPRESCU

...Turner's imagination could distil from light and colour poetry as delicate as that of Shelley. Such are the pale, opalescent visions of rivers and estuaries of which perhaps the most beautiful are those which take their point of departure from Morham Castle. To say that they represent Morham Castle is as misleading as to say that a picture by Braque represents a woman at a piano. The logical connexion between what we should have seen if we had been there and the faint touches of pink, blue, and yellow with which Turner has stained his canvas exists — it is the essence of their beauty — but is extremely complex, and could only be discovered by reliving Turner's experience. And it is inseparable from the technique by which he floats on to the canvas the most delicate films and mists of colour, a technique which Turner, by elaborate precautions, kept a secret in his own day, and which has remained a secret ever since.

KENNETH CLARK

Turner is the last victim, and the most illustrious one, of this need to force the language of painting, which Rembrandt and Velázquez give soul and wings to, letting the painting follow their objective vision and uniting it without effort with their imaginary world. His wish certainly exceeds by far the sentimental wellbeing and peaceful positivism of the other English painters. He is almost the only one to have seen the sulphur sun emerging from the depth of vapours. Only to him was revealed the livid stream, through the veil of smoke hovering in the air. He perceived big phantoms in the mist and the rain, towers of ancient brick and stone, ships, black chimneys, red lanterns piercing the confused dimness, just as a stifled scream bursts out of a vast murmur, to be drowned in it instantly. He felt the sea and the light of the tropics penetrate the dark town, together with the tarred ships and their sails, the wayward flight of the seagulls, the phosphorescent mud, and he mingled with their effaced traces the indistinct echoes of the streets fading away in the distance, the docks, the slums, the parks, the colour of turbid emerald, full of trees and flocks. And, with a lyrical effort of amazing courage, he tried to transfer that intricate and magnificent matter into an imaginary world in which he rose so high that the too rarefied air could not sustain his flight. He was like a bird flying through flashes of lightning, intoxicated with electric storms, blinded by the light. Whether living on this earth or in history, or wandering with Shakespeare through ancient and Romanesque Italy, or plunging with Van Goyen into the bright mists, or visiting with Homer the old heroic universe where the volcano flames and the syrens' song take Ulysses over the Ocean fortuitously, or helping the shipwrecked from a fishing boat, his breath taken away by the wind, soaked with brine and drenched by the rain, or accompanying Nelson in the roar of the cannons, among the smoky clouds, among the fluttering banners, among the rent big sails, wherever the sea water, the sky water and the sun blend, he lives in a realm of supernatural legend, in an aerial palace borne by bleeding shadows and glittering opals, sapphires and rubies.

ÉLIE FAURE

The solid architectures have become translucid spectres behind the fantastic mist which hardly allows anything to be seen of the English land except flitting glimpses, sometimes supernatural, when the moon rises or when the evening light, streaming through a narrow chink in the water veil, reveals to us the top of a tower hanging up among clouds, the bright rotation of a lighthouse, the dark, burning globe sinking gradually. Everything becomes unreal, remote, like that water in which Claude's sun casts off, before disappearing, its streak of liquid purple. He alone reigns from morning till night, fills up the world, fills up history, explodes and spreads out over them in wreaths of flame and blood. The shallow harmonies in which the English painters, after Van Dyck, used to waste their virtuosities, were bound to come to this strange art of Turner's which amounts to the ultimate separation of form from colour, to the evasion of painting into solitary space, detached from any material support, from any visible volume, from any connexion with the sensuous world. After all, this sky and this water merging into each other and melting on the incandescent flame conceal an obvious coolness of meaning, a complete failure to grasp and to convey the trunk and the intermediary branches that link together forever and render sensitive to each other and through each other the roots of man and the perfume of his spirit.

ÉLIE FAURE

As early as 1814 he was moved to paint the *Eruption of the Island of St Vincent at Midnight*, a fire in the flood to lick all rivals, now unfortunately lost. And the subject of one of the greatest of his late, unexhibited pictures is *A Fire at Sea*, where, for once, even the group of figures is successful, and the drawing is fused with the colour of the heat of Turner's imagination. Nothing in romantic painting, it seems to me, is more breath-taking than the passage from the menacing leaden sky on the left to the shower of golden sparks on the right, which burst upon us like some glorious last movement, so that we want to stamp and clap our hands.

KENNETH CLARK

The important element of each painting however is light and its most powerful source for our planet, that is the sun. All that can be imagined as picturesque and dramatic effect, starting from the surrounding world and based on light, was achieved by Turner in such a way that he remains to this day not only one of the greatest artists of Europe, but also a prodigious psychological phenomenon.

G. OPRESCU

In the park and surrounding country he painted some of the most extreme and rapturous of all his sunsets; but even more extraordinary is the series of studies which he made inside the house, in which he recorded in a kind of colour shorthand every incident of these delightful days. They show the certainty with which, by this time, Turner could find a colour equivalent for every form. The culmination of these studies is the famous work known as the *Interior of Petworth* which, although it is not a landscape, may detain us for a minute, as it is the first attempt to make light and colour alone the basis of a design. In this respect it goes further than any of the impressionists, for while they took as their point of departure the natural vision, and are constantly referring back to it, Turner has retained only such elements of the scene as were necessary to his new creation.

KENNETH CLARK

Interior of Tintern Abbey   *Salisbury Cathedral*

Turner hides his scantiness of colour behind fireworks. Light blinds him. He can see nothing apart from it. Everything that is brightened by it has disappeared. Light itself, a miracle, avenges the forsaken earth and the ignored heaven. The world's great harmonious unity breaks down in parts and quakes everywhere. Lost among these precious stones, broken up by these reflections of imaginary fires, the earth loses its consistence, the air thickens, whatever is hard becomes fluid, whatever is fluid becomes compact, the planes overlap, the values mix up, the dismembered universe floats like a bright smoke, shredded by the wind. The poetic and sentimental emotion, definitely superior to the means of expression, disappear almost entirely and can only touch those who have not learned to understand the language of painting. Turner demonstrates the lyrical grandeur of the English soul and at the same time the failure of the English painting to communicate it.

ÉLIE FAURE

The fundamental theme of Turner's poetic feelings was to demonstrate how one can "see" by traversing the large masses of light and shade. He appears thus not only as the forerunner of certain spiritual values of the impressionists, but he also achieves the great historic synthesis between the landscape tradition of the Dutch school and the universal solemnity of classicism.

GIUSEPPE GATT

Turner has confirmed to us its value *(the analysis of shades*, ed.) as a device, but not as a truth . . .

CAMILLE PISSARRO

They *(Monet and Pissarro*, ed.) are amazed at the prestige and the fairy-like magnificence of his colour; . . .First of all they are struck by the effects of snow and ice. They are astounded by the way he succeeded in rendering the feeling of snow whiteness which they had failed to attain until then with their ordinary patches of silvery white flatly displayed . . . And they find that this wonderful result is obtained not by means of a a uniform white but thanks to strokes of various colours, placed side by side and reconstructing from a distance the desired effect.

PAUL SIGNAC

Words are not accurate enough, nor delicate enough to express or trace the constant, all-pervading influence of the finer and vaguer shadows throughout his works, that thrilling influence which gives to the light they leave, its passion and its power. There is not a stone, not a leaf, not a cloud, over which light is not felt to be actually passing and palpitating before our eyes. There is the motion, the actual wave and radiation of the darted beam — not the dull universal daylight, which falls on the landscape without life, or direction or speculation, equal on all things and dead on all things; but the breathing, animated, exulting light, which feels, and receives, and rejoices, and acts — which chooses one thing and rejects another — which seeks, and finds, and loses again — leaping from rock to rock, from leaf to leaf, from wave to wave, — glowing, or flashing, or scintillating, according to what it strikes, or in its holier moods, absorbing and enfolding all things in the deep fulness of its repose, and then again losing itself in bewilderment, and doubt, and dimness; or perishing and passing away, entangled in drifting mist, or melted into melancholy air, but still, — kindling, or declining, sparkling or still, it is the living light, which breathes in its deepest, most entranced rest, which sleeps but never dies.

JOHN RUSKIN

. . .he has attained a high and matchless perfection in watercolours.

The watercolour that allows the white of the paper to be perceived, thus confers to the painting an unusual transparency. Spread over the moistened paper, the light, the blue and violet of the distant mountains, the brightness of the sky in the twilight, the dampness of the atmosphere can be better rendered. Some of Turner's watercolours are painted on moistened paper, so that the outlines of things dissolve into an ethereal veil. Turner applied the devices of the watercolour to his oils as well, using for the latter the sketchy outline, the suggestion already known by the Chinese landscape painters.

M. ALPATOV

In the vast range of his work Turner fulfils practically every aim which the earlier romantics foreshadowed. He is penetrated by a sense of nature's unsubduable, destructive force. If, in front of his great machines, we are tempted to think that his whirlwinds and avalanches are mere rhetoric, later pictures like *After the Deluge* and the *Slave Ship* prove that we were wrong: that Turner's deluges are as truly expressive of his spirit as are those of Leonardo.

KENNETH CLARK

Turner might have said like Cézanne in his last years: "Je deviens, comme peintre, plus lucide devant la nature". This applies particularly to the series of pictures of a stormy sea coast which he painted out of his lodging-house window in Margate. Although not a single form is defined, they are extraordinarily true . . .

KENNETH CLARK

The painters of former times could express *the quality* of the sky, they failed to grasp *the truth* through ignoring the calculated connexion that exists between the blueness of the atmosphere and the whiteness of the clouds, the strict order whereby they fall into three regions, into *three scenic systems*, each answering a specific formal datum: a central region, the only one to have retained the attention of older painters, and particularly that of the Dutch masters: the upper region of which Turner was to make his favourite domain "showing the world another celestial Apocalypse . . ." ★

HUBERT DAMISCH

For many a year we have heard nothing with respect to the works of Turner but accusations of their want of *truth*. To every observation on their power, sublimity, or beauty, there has been but one reply: They are not like nature. I therefore took my opponents on their own ground, and demonstrated, by thorough investigation of actual facts, that Turner *is* like nature, and paints more of nature than any man who ever lived . . .

Turner's system is the closest and most studied approach to truth . . .

The zealous care with which Turner endeavoured to do his duty is proved by a series of large drawings, treating not only directions of line, but effects of light, with a care and completion which should put the work of any ordinary teacher to utter shame . . .

For the conventional colour he substituted a pure straightforward rendering of fact, as far as was in his power; and that not of such fact as had been before

★ Ruskin

Female Academy

Glass Balls, Partly Filled with Water

The Evil Spirit

The Phantom Ship

even suggested, but of all that is *most* brilliant, beautiful, and inimitable; he went to the cataract for its iris, to the conflagration for its flames, asked of the sea its intensest azure, of the sky its clearest gold. For the limited space and defined forms of elder landscape, he substituted the quantity and the mystery of the vastest scenes of earth.

JOHN RUSKIN

His advance into a world of his own creation was made by an infinity of research into the phenomenon of light. "The author" was not only "in this storm"; he was on deck, lashed by the sailors to the mast, to be able to record with his pencil the awfulness of the scene about him.

PHILIP HENDY

He was haunted by the idea that the most illustrious artists of all schools, even the Venetians, had come short of the pure and gay resplendance of nature, on the one hand through the conventional darkening of the shade and on the other hand through their failure to convey the whole light that creation showed them in all its freshness. That is why he tried the brightest and strangest colourings.

THÉOPHILE SILVESTRE

. . .from such notations were created pictures belonging to his later years where shapes seem to dissolve into waves of coloured transparency, in dazzling plays of luminous waves. His virtuosity has no bounds. From blue tones to green tones, from tones of red to tones of yellow, light itself is ever present, and he sets singing in front of us, in long modulations, in flitting sparklings, in moire iridescences, its seducing virtues.

AURÉLIEN DIGEON

His painting embarks upon a kind of dream-vision populated by the colour of the clouds only, ever more abstract, and affords us, beyond any doubt, the first example of pure painting twenty years before the impressionists, penetrating fully into the realm of ambiguous and suggestive imagination which will be illustrated in the mid 20th century by the tachists and a great many masters of lyrical abstraction.

GEORGES PEILLEX

. . .starting by imitating Lorrain and by describing almost photographically the English Gothic in his reproductions of abbeys and dilapidated castles, he had reached that fantastic dissolution of shapes into light which consumes any substance in the pure radiation of immateriality. How exactly such an evolution took place we can observe in his progress from the ideal or idealized nature in the spirit of Poussin, Claude and the Italians, to real, abstract nature, studied and noted as such and, at last, to a new idealization or supernaturalization of sensible nature in a powerful lyrical transmutation which the painting brings to the point of incandescence, as by an alchemic process, when it becomes pure music, pure poetry, without however ceasing to be, essentially, a magnificent *pictorial* achievement.

MARCEL BRION

Turner . . . had visions of a fantastic world bathed in light and resplendent with beauty, but it was a world not of calm but of movement, not of simple harmonies but of dazzling pageantries. He crowded into his pictures every effect which could make them more striking and more dramatic, and, had he been a lesser artist than he was, this desire to impress the public might well have had a disastrous result. Yet he was such a superb stagemanager, he worked with such gusto and skill that he carried it off and the best of his pictures do, in fact, give us a conception of the grandeur of nature at its most romantic and sublime.

E. H. GOMBRICH

Turner's success was also somehow diminished by Ruskin's sublime but excessive and sometimes inexact praises and the significance of his production — greater than that of any other British painter — made the study of his work very difficult. For that reason and for many other reasons, and despite the more and more frequent attitude of seeing in Turner the only master of the English school to have won a place among the great masters of European painting, there is still a huge discrepancy between his fabulous force and the degree of attention given to him by art historians in their studies.

J. ROTHENSTEIN

Turner went even further: the streaming freshness, the silvery brooks, the waves reminiscent of Corot's *Baigneuses*, led with him to a total evaporation. He makes fluid all that is solid, he seeks refuge in the mist of the North, docile to all the currents of the atmosphere, scintillating in its drops with all the quiverings of light. The latent forces underlying Corot's whole work come to life here and sometimes break loose to vex the sea, to quicken the storms and their vortices. Everything moves along and fades out; the solid objects have lost their consistence; what is left is only mirages and glimpses of sparkles through evaporations.

Thus, as has been often stated, Turner asserts himself as a forerunner of Impressionism which, taking a step forward in the frenzy of dematerialization, attained the stage of pure light, retaining from the compact universe only the pretexts simplified to a reflection or a vibration.

RENÉ HUYGHE

Denying the tradition of *opus anglicanum* and of the Gothics, seeking to identify himself with the elements, he advanced ever more boldly, from one painting to another, towards the substantiation of his own original vision of objects floating in the iridescent light, losing their contours, melting down into it, so much so that of his landscape hardly anything distinct is left but the looming of I don't know what sparkling phantoms in which we perceive the three qualities which the great statesman Edmund Burke gave as corollaries of the sublime: grandeur, awe and infinitude.

PIERRE COURTHION

His romanticism is absolute and in this sense his egocentrism is imbued with a lyricism which will impart to his most characteristic and most contested work a vertigo and an ecstasy of colour which painting had never experienced before.

MAURICE RAYNAL

Turner discovered and conveyed on to canvas, in the manner of a visionary, the extraordinary subtlety of the British isles, with its three components: the sun, the sea and the mist. The twilight and the aurora appear on Turner's canvases as mysterious supraterrestrial phenomena. The colours melt into phantastic tones, the shapes fade into barely visible contours. It is a dreamland, a fairyland as we have never seen in painting before, in none of the pictures in the great art galleries of the world.

DUMITRU POPESCU

I do not know a landscape painter in the world even if I were to mention Ruysdael or Claude Lorrain, to have been able to revive on canvas reality with so much charm and with such an etherialized harmony.

C. DE MARTINO

He was a genius not only in the volume and energy of his work, but also in its inexhaustibility as a source of fresh experience.

GRAHAM REYNOLDS

CHRONOLOGY
AND CONCORDANCES

1775   Son of a barber and wig maker and grandson of a butcher, Joseph Mallord Turner is born on April 23, in Maiden Lane, Covent Garden, London.

1776   *John Constable, the great landscape painter and the artist's secret rival, is born at East Bergholt, a village in Suffolk.*

1785   A frail, sickly nature stifled by the tortuous and morally uncertain family life and above all weighed down by his mother's neurosis, he leaves the "well bottom" of his home and, with his father's help, goes to live with his uncle at Brentford, where he learns to read and write.

1787   The artist's precocious abilities are obvious. At the age of 12 he produces drawings and watercolours— most of them reproductions from memory — after various engravings. Astonishing, even at this early stage, are the sense of detail, the precision of forms and his capacity to organize a whole.

1788   Goes to school at Margate. He is only 13 when, powerfully impressed by the sea, he produces two watercolours significant for the nature and evolution of his art. It is the moment which will strengthen his father's faith, unshaken up to his death, in his son's vocation as an artist. Contributing to it were also the results obtained by the pupil in the studio of Thomas Malton, author of watercolours with topographical and architectural topics.

Birth of Byron.

1789   Is accepted as a student at the Royal Academy. Then for a short period he lives at Sunningwell, a place between Abingdon and Oxford.

William Blake engraves and publishes his book of poems Songs of Innocence.

1790   Exhibits for the first time. During a trip he stops at Bristol where he visits John Narraway, a friend of his father's.

1792   Exhibits at the Academy *Malmesbury Cathedral* and *The Pantheon, the morning after the fire.*

1793   Visits Oxford and Kent, and a year later the Peak District and the Midlands. He produces, according to tradition, a great many topographical drawings and engravings.

1794—95 This period is marked by his need for scope, for inner confrontation, his devouring wish to minutely study and examine the masterpieces of Claude Lorrain, Poussin, Salvator Rosa, Van der Velde, Ruysdael.

1795   Enters into the artistic atmosphere in the house of the illustrious Dr. Monroe, a philantropist generous to young talents, where, besides the exhilarating presence of Girtin, a brilliant and inspired creator of landscapes, bearing a direct influence on his painting, he discovers Cozens' work.

1796   Achieves the painting, *Fishermen at sea*, a marine in which one can foreseee the artist's great chromatic obsession to come.

Birth of Corot.

1797   Exhibits his first oil, *Bridgewater Sea Piece*, at the Royal Academy.
The fantastic visionary poet Coleridge writes The Rime of the Ancient Mariner, a vision in a dream.

1798   Composes another marine, *Buttermere, Lake with part of Cromackwater, Cumberland, a shower* in which the explosive, tumultuous light floods the landscape and under its phosphorecent aura brings out in full relief the minutest details. At the exhibition, he attaches mottoes to his works from Thompson's *The Seasons*, from Wordsworth and Coleridge's *Lyrical Ballads*—a volume which had just come out — and from Milton. The quotations are poetic hints to the effects of light and atmosphere. One of them, from Milton, begins with words which supply the chief motif of Turner's mature work: "*Ye mists and exhalations that now rise/ From hill or streaming lake.*"

Birth of Delacroix.

1799   Completes the watercolour *Norham Castle* which, though tributary to the topographical landscape style then in the fashion, represents, through the rigour of its construction, an important landmark in the development of his art. He is tormented by the secret, then gradually more manifest, ambition to challenge and to excel Claude Lorrain.

Birth of Honoré de Balzac.

1800   Works feverishly at "marines", castles, landscapes of Scotland and Wales with amazing skill which would not disappoint a public yearning for picturesque details, for a romantic atmosphere and even for the savour of anecdote. His success increases considerably . He paints at the same time *Aeneas and the Sibyl, Lake Avernus,* where he associates the classical rigour of landscape and characters — in Lorrain's style — with the presence of the solar gold, voluptuously irradiative. His sense of architectural values is equally expressed in his work *The fifth plague of Egypt.* In fact the theme is the seventh plague, as is revealed by the quotation printed in the catalogue: "The Lord sent thunder and hail and the fire ran along the ground."

1802   At the age of 27 is elected a member of the Royal Academy. He paints, having a few elements in common with Poussin's style, *The tenth plague of Egypt.*
His first journey abroad, visiting Paris and Switzerland. At the Louvre he is attracted by the paintings of the great landscape artists Ruysdael or Poussin and he cannot refrain from some shrewd and competent remarks full of subtlety. He makes a great number of sketches after Raphael, Correggio, Guercino, Domenichino and Titian. Also impressed by the Alpine landscape, which, he writes: 'On the whole it surpasses Wales, and Scotland too.' Dating from this period are the paintings *Fishermen upon a lee-shore, in squally weather* (in which a vexed sea, reproduced from a prodigious memory, already reveals the artist's pictorial qualities and dramatic instinct) and the famous *Calais Pier, with French poissards preparing for sea: an English packet arriving* — a convulsive and very precise representation of the sea's rage, of the Cyclopean torment of the waves, coming from the artist's direct experience.

Birth of Victor Hugo.

1805   The year of the second large canvas of marine inspiration, *The Shipwreck.*

Birth of John Keats.

1806   Exhibits in unfinished form the topical painting *The Battle of Trafalgar,* an attempt to bring successfully to the foreground the subtly orchestrated pictorial values.

W.E. Wells, the artist's friend, founds the "Water-Colour Society".

1807   Exhibits the oils *The Thames near Windsor* and *Eton, from the River.* It is now too that he finishes *The Thames near Walton Bridge.*

1808   Presents in a final form *The Battle of Trafalgar, as seen from the mizen starboard shrouds of the 'Victory',* at the British Institution.
With this serious approach of immediate history, perhaps even before, the artist leaves for a time his "marines" and takes refuge in a series of calm experiences, in paintings of genre, reminiscent somehow of Dutch painting, with soft éclairages, with mannerist transparences and symetries: *The Sun rising through vapour, A Country Blacksmith disputing the price of Iron, and the price charged to the butcher for shoeing hispony, The Cobbler's Home, Frosty Morning.*
John Leicester invites him to paint his Cheshire residence, Tabley House.

1809   Finishes the painting *Crew weighing anchor* and executes two works for Lord Lonsdale of Westmorland.

Philipp Otto Runge begins the painting the Great Morning, *left unfinished, "One of the most delightful and astounding masterpieces of German Romantic painting" (M.Brion).*

1810   *Goethe publishes his famous treatise* Zur Farbenlehre. *The Hamburg publisher Perthes prints Runge's* Treatise on colours, *entitled "The sphere of colours or building the relations and blends of colours and their full affinity with a corresponding attempt at establishing harmony in the manner of arranging those colours".*

Turner visits his collector Fawkes at Farnley Hall. According to some biographers, during this period he breaks off his relations with Sarah Danley.

1811   After moving to Hammersmith Mall in 1807, attracted by the landscapes of the Thames, he now settles at Sion Ferry House, in Isleworth.

1812   *Cottage destroyed by an Avalanche,* an hallucinating projection of an Alpine disaster.
The grandiose "Snowstorm" called *Hannibal and his Army Crossing the Alps* contradicts and at the same time confirms him: "Besides a return to an apocalyptic vision, we are now in the presence of a composition not only awe-inspiring, but in which the awe-inspiring effect assumes a terrifying character. Space errupts and overflows both himself and everybody" (J.J. Mayoux). In the catalogue to the exhibition he publishes the first lines of his bitter composition *The Errors of Hope.* Finishes *Devonshire, fishing at sea in a storm.*

At the same exhibition John Martin is also present with Sadak.

Byron writes Childe Harold.

1813   Exhibits *Frosty Morning,* "an absolute protest against the labelling of landscape as map-making". (G. Reynolds).

1814   Though Lorrainian in style, the picture *Appullia in search of Appullus* asserts the artist's great personality.

1815   *Dido building Carthage*; or *the rise of The Carthaginian Empire* represents stylistically an apogee: a true pictorial poem of the sea and the clouds.
In presenting it to the National Gallery, the artist expresses his wish (eventually granted) that it should be exhibited beside Claude Lorrain's *The Seaport. Crossing the brook* is nearer the painting of genre but here too his characteristic colour modulations surprise due to their freshness.

1817   *Saint Ursula boarding the ship*, a canvas also achieved in the spirit of the French master, treated however with a greater potentiality of light, like *The Decline of the Carthaginian Empire* as well.

Keats writes his first book of poems: "Poems by John Keats".

1818   *John Keats publishes the allegoric poem* Endymion.

1819   First journey to Italy.
Composes the landscape *Raby Castle.*
Leaves unfinished the group of the 70 engravings *Liber Studiorum,* entitled after the manner of Lorrain and achieved over a number of years. From Italy he returns with almost 1500 drawings in pencil or pen. Insignificant as regards oil paintings, the journey is repeated four times, with visits to Venice, Turin, Como, Genoa, Milan, Bologna, Rimini, Orvieto, Ancona, Florence, Naples.
The most significant gain of the period between 1819 and 1840, called "intermediary" is, together with a continuous decantation of light, with its freshness, transparency and purity, the imperceptible evanescence of form, absorbed and transposed into ineffability.
Another significant landscape: *England: Richmond Hill on the Prince Regent's Birthday.*

1820   Turner composes a new "Snowstorm": *The Passage of Mont Cenis,* together with *Forum Romanum: The Arch of Titus,* and *Rome, from the Vatican: Raffaello, accompanied by La Fornarina, preparing his Pictures for the decoration of the Loggia.*

John Keats publishes, among others, his great odes, poems of supreme Romantic concentration: To a Nightingale *and* On a Grecian Urn.
Shelley finishes the eruptive confession dedicated to mankind's ideal of freedom: Prometheus Unbound.

1820—21   *The obsession of fulgurous, volatile, ethereal matter preoccupies Constable too, who creates a great many "studies of clouds", "studies of the sky", exercises in blue and white, fugitive, passionate, penetrating intuitions of nature in motion. It is difficult, the artist confesses, "to name a type of landscape in which the sky should not impose its note, should not determine the range of values, should not be the main organ of feeling."*

1821   *Constable composes the canvas* The Hay Wain.

1822   *Death of Percy Bysshe Shelley.*
Birth of Baudelaire and Dostoiewsky.
Wilkie exhibits the painting, greatly appreciated by Géricault, The Chelsea Invalids reading "the Gazette" after the Battle of Waterloo.

1823   On the occasion of the exhibition, Turner presents, among others: *The bay of Baiae — with Apollo and Sibyl* and, in a vast, magnificent version, *The Battle of Trafalgar* — a moving expression of the artist's highly patriotic virtues, his sensibility implanted in the living contemporary world.

1824   *Death of Lord Byron.*
Constable paints the canvas of great power of expression: Coalers of Brighton harbour.
The year of the famous Paris Salon where Constable has a resounding success. Astonished, the legend goes, at the vibration of his colouring, Delacroix wholly repainted his canvas The Massacre at Chios.

1825   In the summer Turner visits Holland, Belgium and northern Germany.

1826   *Constable completes his most popular landscape creation:* The Cornfield.

Turner returns to France and Germany in order to explore the landscapes of the rivers Meuse and Moselle.

Descending from the suite of disciples of the visionary Blake, the artist Palmer assimilates Turner's overwhelming influence and achieves, beginning with this period, some canvases which represent a landmark in the history of English landscape: Valley with brilliant Cloud, The Magic Apple. *With hallucinatory symbolism, with reminiscences of cabal, mysticism, astrology, gnostic philosophy, William Blake marks a significant moment by his engravings and tempera paintings, in a very personal interpretation:* Satan covering Job with Pustules *or his illustrations to Dante's* Divine Comedy.

1827   Cromwell, *Victor Hugo's resounding drama, is published.*
Death of William Blake.

1828   *The life of the charming, fascinating aquarellist Bonington ends suddenly.*

Turner exhibits *East Cowes Castle, the seat of J. Nash, Esq; the Regatta beating to windward* at the Royal Academy, and similarly, *East Cowes Castle; the Regatta starting for their moorings.*
Paints *View of Orvieto* at Rome.

1829   Creates the masterpiece *Ulysses deriding Polyphemus*, which comes as a powerful shock to critical opinion. Beyond the mythological anecdote or some classic-like harmonies, the picture impresses through the triumphal, awe-inspiring sonority of Wagnerian apotheosis, made more diaphanous though, lined with gold and purple.

Death of the artist's father.

1830   *Pilate washing his hands* already introduces some nuances of the tonality and atmosphere of the Petworth "interiors". Lord Egremont invites him to live at his castle at Petworth. *Interior at Petworth*, through its atmosphere of strange nonreality, through the diffuse chromatic onomatopoeia of colour tints, incandescent eddies — and beside which the tones of yellow especially, then of orange, red, amber and green are so disposed as to make a final attack on the mystery — attains the highest peak of his pictorial decantation. The most significant in the series of his celebrated "Interiors" is his painting in the Tate Gallery.
Music party, Petworth is composed in a similar register (one of his biographers, Graham Reynolds, as well as Finberg, proposed as date 1830, the National Gallery catalogue of "the English School" suggests the year 1835). Impressionistic *avant la lettre*, the picture is also an "interior" with an atmosphere created by sounds, recollected, a musical metaphor which, paradoxically, the violent tones of red and black render even more reposeful and profound.
Decorates Roger's volume *Italy.*

1832   *Staffa: Fingal's Cave.* With echoes from his rough marines, the picture presents especially the atmosphere and an inward interpretation of the latent dynamics of Neptune's realm.

1834   *The burning of the Houses of Lords and Commons* is a waterscape with backround broad brushstrokes of a dingy bluish-green, with gradations of colour towards livid and yellow, cleft by a hallucinating diagonal mass of shredded red, beyond which the walls of the building looming phantomatically enhance the uncanny atmosphere.
A Fire at Sea expresses a feeling of dumb terror in face of the disaster.
Achieves the designs for Byron's poems published by Murray and the vignettes for Roger's volume *Poems.*

Carlyle publishes his celebrated essay Sartor Resartus.
Death of Coleridge on July 25.
Birth of James Abbot McNeill Whistler.

1835   *A Vaulted Hall*, dated 1835—1840, is strikingly modern: wrapped in a long wave of steamy-phosphorescent light, the human figures step forth, forming an insubstantial cortège beneath a range of vaults rigorously drawn.
Seascape, also dated 1835—1840, offers the same air of transparency and fluidity of watercolours. Here the yellow raises above the water a mysterious horizon, dramatized by the dark brownish tincture stroke of the jet of shade, of the hallucinating waterspout on the left of the picture foreshadowing by its abstract structure some of the representations in Henry Michaux's lithographs today.
Two Women and a Letter, belonging approximately to the year 1835, reconstructs in fact the atmosphere at Petworth. The white of the woman in the middle has a spectral tormenting air, giving consistency and solidity to the figure down left, which might be the production of a French impressionist.
Dinner in a Great Room with Figures in Costume. The construction of the picture is strangely syncretic, reminding allusively of the Rembrantesque lesson of light and shade but foreshadowing the later technical subtleties of the impressionists and neoimpressionists.
Open air theatre, Venice and *Figures on a bridge, Venice* demonstrate the truth that Turner allows more and more his shapes to be absorbed by colour, by the magic of tones.

1835—1840 Finishes *Ponte delle Torri, Spoleto*, an astounding experiment in transfiguring the elements: the bridge is scarcely visible through a diaphanously violet haze beneath a vague sun, like a golden echo in the vastness of the sky.

1836   Exhibits *Juliet and her Nurse.* Though highly controversial, the picture is no less famous for its strange halo of light and for its lyricism and tragic reverberations.

1837   *The parting of Hero and Leander*, subtitled 'from the Greek of Musaeus', displays, besides a remarkable sense of volumes, the refined richness of colour. Owing to colours, Rothenstein says, Turner "expresses perfectly the struggling force of the sea and the sky dominating and devouring the flimsy hopes of an ephemeral mankind".
Snowstorm, avalanche, and inundation is the pathetic metaphor of a cosmic outburst of elements against elements, of a lurid apocalyptic eruption, blind and destructive, against nature herself.

Death of Constable.
His friend, Lord Egremont, dies in November.

1838   *The Fighting 'Temeraire' tugged to her last berth to be broken up.* Born from the artist's polemic intention to demonstrate in Ruskin's spirit the naïve scorn for the bourgeois "industrialism" and positivism of his time, the picture proposes the shocking comparison between two vessels, an old sailor, haloed with magnificence and glory (she had taken part in the battle of Trafalgar) and the new tug, dark and mean, an expression of the new technique, made to be the sea "grave digger" of the former.

Birth of Nicolae Grigorescu.
Delacroix paints Chopin's portrait.
Chevreul writes his work: On the law of the simultaneous contrast of colours.

Turner studies thoroughly and annotates *Zur Farbenlehre* by Goethe, published in Eastlake's English translation.

1840 *Norham Castle, Sunrise* is a landscape reduced to its essentials made up of extremely fine sulphur-like irradiations, with gradations of colour towards a transparent pale blue encircling a tiny bluish nucleus, a suggestion of the castle hovering in dream and legend.
Composes *The Evening Star*, an elaborate study of constellations irradiating light in the dusk.
Slavers throwing overboard the dead and dying — Typhoon coming on is a tragic and terrifying vision in Melville's spirit where suffering becomes an atrocious nightmare of cosmic dimensions: over the epidemic causing the throwing of the negro slaves' corpses overboard, through the wrath of the ruthless typhoon, monsters in a turmoil and swarming strange shapes beset the ship with its masts of a putrid purple colour piercing the sky fallen like a red shroud over the infernal scene. "Never was Turner's imagination so 'fantastic' in inventing shapes and in using colours." (M.Brion).
Rockets and blue lights (close at hand) to warn steamboats of shoal water — a marine scene in which the storm becomes a medium for luminiscent effects, for terrible "correspondences" between the phosphorescent foaming crests and the air burning beyond the masts. The painting is exhibited at the Clark Institute of Williamstown.

Birth of Monet, Odilon Redon, Rodin.
1841 *Death of the Victorian artist David Wilkie.*

1842 *Snowstorm — steamboat off a harbour's mouth making signals in shallow water, and going by the lead,* exhibited at the Royal Academy, in a violently straightforward marine, Turner, recording with his proverbial sensitive memory his own anxiety on board the *Ariel* where, as he himself confesses, in order to experience the blinding spectacle of the seastorm, the burning lightning, the howling waves, in order to recreate everything in one vision, he tied himself to the mast. Overwhelmed by the genuine dramatism of the work, by the extraordinary movement of the sea, Ruskin confesses that the artist has surpassed everything that had been composed in landscape on that theme.
Peace, burial at sea is a composition of trenchant symbolism, a clear suggestion of the mourning which, through the strips of smoke and the ship's shadows, is reflected diffusively in the sky and sea.

1843 *Shade and darkness — the evening of the Deluge.* Tormented by the "mystery" of colour, Turner keeps experimenting, abstracting the colours with a visionary's ever fresh instinct, and produces baffling renewing aspects.
Light and colour (Goethe's Theory) — the morning after the Deluge (left with important annotations by the artist) is a painting purified from all sensorial charge: the eddy of light is the light of interiority, of our burning latencies, consumming themselves in dramatically tormenting questions.

John Ruskin publishes the first volume of the series Modern Painters.

1844 *Rain, Steam and Speed—The Great Western Railway* is a brilliant synthesis of the landscapist's virtues, of his colour magic, of his power to grasp and render the poetic ineffability of things. A new type of the sublime, the author seems to suggest to us, asserts its domination, the modern sublime, an expression of a new existential rhythm, of new spiritual dynamics. The painting may be considered, just like Monet's *Impression, soleil levant,* the birth certificate of Impressionism.

1845 Travels to Dieppe and Tréport to contemplate "storms and sunsets". Composes the evocative sketches *Coach at Eu* and *Interior of Church.*

1846 Exhibits *Whalers (boiling Blubber) entangled in Flaw Ice, endeavouring to extricate themselves* (created a year before), two "Venetian scenes" and *Undine giving the ring to Masaniello, Fisherman of Naples.*
Has the apocalyptic vision of *The Angel standing in the Sun,* a strange tourbillon-like circular composition.

1848 *Dante Gabriel Rossetti, helped by William Holman Hunt and John Everet Millais, creates the artistic movement "The Pre-Raphaelite Brotherhood."*
Birth of Gauguin.

1849 *The first Pre-Raphaelite exhibition, with works by Rossetti, Hunt and Millais.*

1850 *Death of Balzac.*
The two first issues of the Pre-Raphaelites' review "The Germ".

1851 Turner dies at the age of 76 on December 19 and is buried in a crypt, beside Reynolds, in St. Paul's Cathedral.

Birth of Ion Andreescu.
Millais exhibits *The Return of the Dove to the Ark.*

BIBLIOGRAPHY

GRAHAM REYNOLDS, *Turner*, Thames and Hudson: London, 1969

Turner, Five Letters and a Postscript by Lewis Hind, London: T.C. & E.C. JACK

MARTIN BUTLIN, *Watercolours from the Turner Bequest* 1818—1845, Tate Gallery

The Tate Gallery edited by Sir Edward J. Poynter, P.R.A., D.C.L., Litt. D., III, Cassell and Company, 1900

T.S.R. BOASE, *Shipwrecks in English Romantic Painting*, "Journal of the Warburg and Courtauld Institutes", XXII, nos. 3—4, 1959

From the Classicists to the Impressionists, III, Selected and Edited by Elisabeth Gilmore Holt, Anchor Books, Doubleday & Co. Inc., Garden City, New York, 1966

WILLIAM GAUNT, *The Observer's Book of Modern Art*, Frederick Warne & Co. Ltd., 1958

WILLIAM GAUNT, *The Observer's Book of Modern Art*, Frederick Warne & Co. Ltd., 1964

PIERRE COURTHION, *Le Romantisme*, Éditions d'Art, Albert Skira, 1961

GIUSEPPE GATT, *Turner*, Editions Flammarion, 1967

JOHN ROTHENSTEIN, *La Tate Gallery*, Editions Aimery Somogy, 1963

AURÉLIEN DIGEON, *L'école anglaise de peinture*, Editions Pierre Tisné

PHILIPP OTTO RUNGE, *La sphère des couleurs*, Critique, Août—Septembre 1973

Encyclopédie des Arts illustrée, préface de Raymond Cogniat, Editions du Livre d'or, Flammarion, 1964

HUBERT DAMISCH, *Théorie du nuage*, Editions du Seuil, 1972

RENÉ HUYGHE, *Les puissances de l'image*, Flammarion, 1965

RENÉ HUYGHE, *Dialogue avec le visible*, Editions Flammarion, 1955

RENÉ HUYGHE, *L'art et l'Homme*, III, Librairie Larousse, 1961

E.H. GOMBRICH, *Art and Illusion*, Phaidon Press, London, 1968

E.H. GOMBRICH, *L'art et son histoire*, Editions René Julliard, 1967

H.W. JANSON, *Histoire de l'Art*, Editions Cercle d'Art, 1970

MAURICE RAYNAL, *De Goya à Gauguin*, Editions d'Art Albert Skira, 1961

GEORGE KENT, *Great Painters and Great Paintings*, The Reader's Digest Association, Pleasantville-Montreal-Sydney

Histoire générale de l'art, Editions Flammarion, 1950

MARCEL PROUST, *Plastiches et mélanges*, Editions Gallimard, 1947

MARCEL PROUST, *Elstir — Despre artă* (Elstir — On Art), texts selected and translated by Paul Dinopol, Meridiane Publishing House, Bucharest, 1970

GEORGES PEILLEX, *La peinture du XIXe siècle*, Pont-Royal, 1964

Peinture éternelle, Editions Pont-Royal, 1957

PHILIP HENDY, *National Gallery*, Editions Aimery Somogy, 1960

HERBERT READ, *The Philosophy of Modern Art*, The World Publishing Company, Cleveland and New York, 1961

HERBERT READ, *Art and Alienation*, Thames and Hudson, 1967

HERBERT READ, *The Meaning of Art*, Pitman, N.Y., 1951

KENNETH CLARK, *Landscape into Art*, John Murray, London, 1952

G. OPRESCU, *Manual de Istoria Artei* (A Handbook of the History of Arts), vol. III, 19th century, Published by "Universul", 1946

DUMITRU POPESCU, *Drumuri europene* (European Roads), Youth Publishing House, 1965

M. ALPATOV, *The History of Art*, vol. II, Romanian edition, Meridiane Publishing House, Bucharest, 1967

ÉLIE FAURE, *Histoire de l'art*, Editions Jean-Jacques Pauvert, Paris

J.J. MAYOUX, *La peinture anglaise*, Paris, 1967

MARCEL BRION, *Peinture romantique*, Albin Michel, 1967

PAUL SIGNAC, *D'Eugène Delacroix au néo-impressionisme*, Paris, Floury, 1934

ERIC PROTTER, *Painters on Painting*, Grosset & Dunlop, London, 1972

LIST OF REPRODUCTIONS

17. STORM CLOUDS, SUNSET
1825
Watercolour over pencil
Tate Gallery

18. FORUM ROMANUM
1826
Oil
Tate Gallery

19. ST. LAURENT
1826—1833
Watercolour and gouache on blue paper
British Museum

20. YACHT RACING IN THE SOLENT
1827
Oil
Tate Gallery

21. BETWEEN DECKS
1827
Oil
Tate Gallery

22. SHIPPING AT COWES
1827
Oil
Tate Gallery

23. ORVIETO
1828
Oil
Tate Gallery

24. ARCHWAY WITH TREES BY THE SEA
1828
Oil
Tate Gallery

25. INTERIOR AT PETWORTH
1830—1837
Oil
Tate Gallery

26. PILATE WASHING HIS HANDS
1830
Oil
Tate Gallery

27. A SHIP AGROUND
1830
Oil
Tate Gallery

28. ROCKETS AND BLUE LIGHTS
1840
Oil
Sterling and Francine Clark
Art Institute, Williamstown,
Massachusetts

29. CHICHESTER CANAL
1830—1831
Oil
Tate Gallery

30. WATTEAU
1831
Oil on panel
Tate Gallery

31. SOUTHERN LANDSCAPE WITH AN AQUEDUCT AND WATERFALL
1830—1835
Oil
Tate Gallery

32. STAFFA: FINGAL'S CAVE
1832
Oil
Gavin Astor Collection

33. VAN TROMP RETURNING AFTER THE BATTLE OFF THE DOGGER BANK
1833
Oil
Tate Gallery

34. A FIRE AT SEA
1834
Oil
National Gallery

35. BRIDGE OF SIGHS. DUCAL PALACE AND CUSTOMS HOUSE, VENICE
Oil
Tate Gallery

36. THE BURNING OF THE HOUSES OF LORDS AND COMMONS.
1834
Oil
John Severance Collection
Cleveland Museum of Art

37. LANDSCAPE WITH WATER
1835—1840
Oil
Tate Gallery

38. SHORE AND SKY, SUNSET
1835
Watercolour over pencil
British Museum

39. TWO WOMEN AND A LETTER
1835
Oil
Tate Gallery

40. THE PONTE DELLE TORRI, SPOLETO
1835—1840
Oil
Tate Gallery

41. THE ARCH OF CONSTANTINE, ROME
1835
Tate Gallery

42. MOONLIGHT ON THE LAGOON, VENICE
1835
Watercolour and gouache
British Museum

43. BOATS AT SEA
1835—1840
Watercolour
British Museum

44. SUNRISE: A CASTLE ON A BAY
1835—1845
Oil
Tate Gallery

45. SNOWSTORM, AVALANCHE, AND INUNDATION
1837
Oil
Art Institute of Chicago

46. THE FIGHTING 'TEMERAIRE' TUGGED TO HER LAST BERTH TO BE BROKEN UP
1838
Oil
National Gallery

47. VENICE: SANTA MARIA DELLA SALUTE
1835
Watercolour and gouache on dark paper
British Museum

48. PHRYNE GOING TO THE PUBLIC
    BATH AS VENUS
    1838
    Oil
    Tate Gallery

49. SLAVERS THROWING OVER—
    BOARD THE DEAD AND DYING.
    TYPHOON COMING ON
    1840
    Oil
    Museum of Fine Arts, Boston

50. NORHAM CASTLE, SUNRISE
    1840—1845
    Oil
    Tate Gallery

51. SUNRISE, WITH SEA MONSTERS
    1840
    Oil
    Tate Gallery

52. BUILDINGS BY A LAKE
    1840—1845
    Watercolour over pencil
    British Museum

53. THE ARSENAL, RIO DI SAN
    DANIELO, VENICE 1840
    1840
    Watercolour
    British Museum

54. SNOWSTORM
    1842
    Oil
    National Gallery

55. EU WITH LOUIS-PHILIPPE'S
    CHÂTEAU
    1845
    Watercolour and red ink over pencil
    British Museum

56. PEACE — BURIAL AT SEA
    (detail)
    1842
    Oil
    Tate Gallery

57. LIGHT AND COLOUR
    1843
    Oil
    Tate Gallery

58. RAIN, STEAM AND SPEED
    1844
    Oil
    National Gallery

59. SKELETON FALLING OFF A HORSE
    1830
    Oil
    Tate Gallery

60. THE ANGEL STANDING IN THE
    SUN
    1846
    Oil
    Tate Gallery

61. THE VISIT TO THE TOMB
    1850
    Oil
    Tate Gallery

62. INTERIOR OF CHURCH
    1845
    Watercolour
    British Museum

1. Portrait of the Artist aged twenty-three

2. Venus and Adonis

3. The Passage of the St. Gothard

6. The Sun Rising through Vapour

9. Crossing the Brook

10. Cottage destroyed by an Avalanche

12. Rome from the Vatican: Raffaelle Accompanied by
La Fornarina, Preparing His Pictures for the Decoration
of the Loggia

16. The Bay of Baiae, with Apollo and Sibyl

17. Storm Clouds, Sunset

18. Forum Romanum

20. Yacht Racing in the Solent

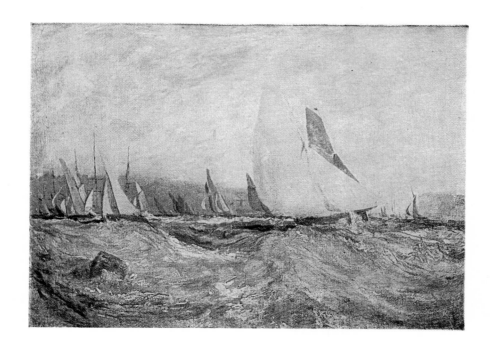

21. Between Decks

22. Shipping at Cowes

24. Archway with trees by the Sea

25. Interior at Petworth

26. Pilate Washing His Hands

27. A Ship Aground
28. Rockets and Blue Lights

29. Chichester Canal
30. Watteau

31. Southern Landscape with an Aqueduct and Waterfall

33. Van Tromp Returning after the Battle off the Dogger Bank

34. A Fire at Sea

35. Bridge of Sighs. Ducal Palace and Customs House, Venice

38. Shore and Sky, Sunset

39. Two Women and a Letter

44. Sunrise: a Castle on Bay

45. Snowstorm, Avalanche, and Inundation

46. The Fighting 'Temeraire' Tugged to her Last Berth
    to be Broken up

48. Phryne going to the Public Bath as Venus

49. Slavers throwing overboard the dead and dying. Typhoon coming on

50. Norham Castle, Sunrise

52. Buildings by a Lake

54. Snowstorm

55. Eu with Louis-Philippe's Château

56. Peace — Burial at Sea, *detail*

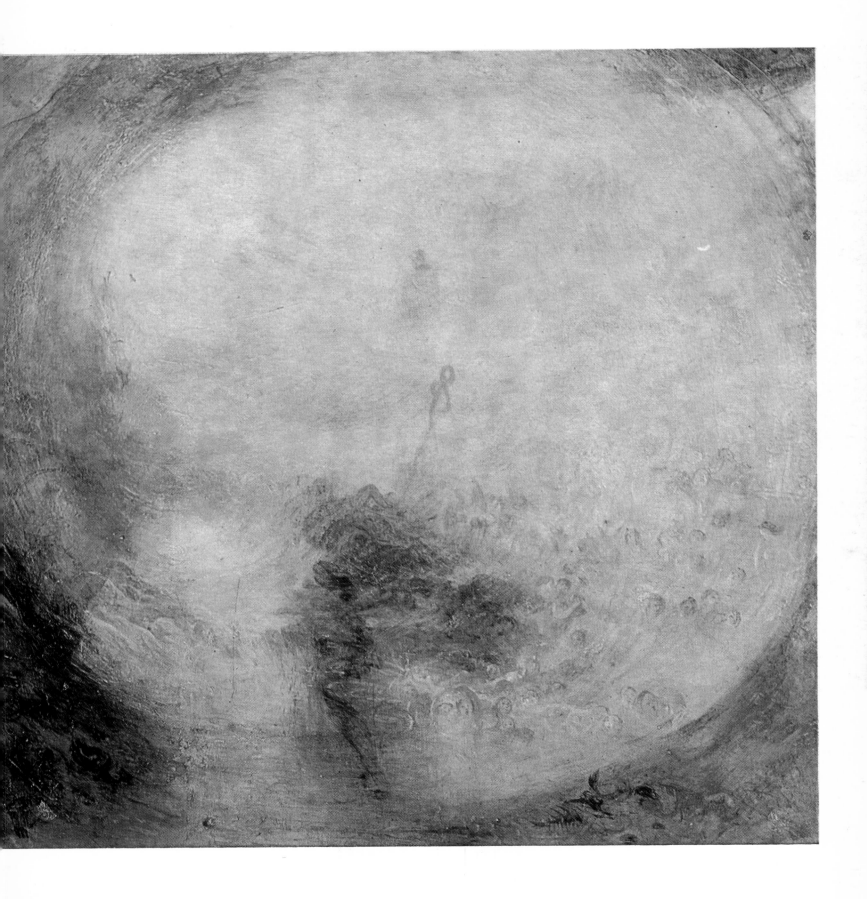

59. Skeleton falling off a Horse

60. The Angel Standing in the Sun

61. The Visit to the Tomb

62. Interior of a Church

ILLUSTRATIONS NOS.

4, 8, 9, 12, 21, 25, 28, 30, 56, 57, 61.
are reproduced by permission of
THE TATE GALLERY, LONDON.

MERIDIANE PUBLISHING HOUSE
BUCHAREST

PRINTED IN ROMANIA